THE MYSTERIES OF THE ROSARY

STEP BY STEP GUIDE TO THE ROSARY PRAYER, JOYFUL, LUMINOUS, SORROWFUL AND GLORIOUS MYSTERIES OF THE ROSARY

Williams Mark

Copyright ©2023 Williams Mark

All rights reserved. No part of these publications may be reproduced, distributed, or transmitted in any form or by any means, including photocopying recording, or other electronic or mechanical methods, without the prior written permission of the publisher, except in the case of brief quotations embodied in critical reviews and certain other noncommercial uses permitted by copyright law.

Dedication

In loving memory of my grandmother, who instilled in me a profound devotion to the Blessed Virgin Mary and the Rosary. Her unwavering faith continues to inspire this work. To all who find solace and spiritual connection through the Mysteries of the Rosary, may this book deepen your understanding and strengthen your faith.

CONTENTS

INTRODUCTION
THE ORIGIN OF THE MYSTERIES OF THE ROSARY.

STEP BY STEP GUIDE FOR PRAYING THE ROSARY.

PRAYERS SAID IN THE ROSARY.

THE MYSTERIES OF THE ROSARY.

WHY DO WE RECITE THE ROSARY.

PRAYING THE ROSARY EVERY DAY

INTRODUCTION

The Rosary is a Scripture-based meditation prayer. When we pray the Rosary, we ask Mary to pray for us while we contemplate the life, death, and resurrection of her son Jesus.

Pope John Paul II stated in his 2002 apostolic letter Rosarium Virginis Mariae that the Rosary allows "the Christian people to sit at the school of Mary and are led to contemplate the beauty on the face of Christ and to experience the depths of his love."

The Rosary is still a popular prayer today. In reaction to the crisis in Ukraine, Pope Francis called for Christians to pray "the Holy Rosary for peace" in May 2022. Archbishop Cordileone of San Francisco encouraged the people to pray a "Rosary for Peace" on Election Day in November 2022.

THE ORIGIN OF THE MYSTERIES OF THE ROSARY

The Mysteries of the Rosary are a precious gift from the Blessed Virgin Mary to the faithful. They help us meditate on the life of Jesus and Mary. The origin of the Mysteries is a story of love, devotion, and a desire to draw closer to God through prayer.

- Early Christian Devotion:

Long ago, Christians used prayer beads to help them recite their prayers. This practice was inspired by the monks who recited the Psalms using beads. It was a way to help people focus their hearts and minds on God.

• Growing Love for Mary:

As time passed, devotion to the Virgin Mary grew. Christians felt a deep love for Mary, the mother of Jesus. They wanted to express their love and honor her. This devotion led to prayers and hymns dedicated to Mary's grace and love.

• The "Psalter of Mary":

In the 12th and 13th centuries, a beautiful tradition called the "Psalter of Mary" emerged. This prayer practice involved saying 150 Hail Mary prayers, just like the 150 Psalms in the Bible. People grouped these prayers into sets of ten, with an Our Father prayer in between. This practice laid the foundation for the Rosary.

- **St. Dominic's Role:**

Though there are different stories about its origin, one tradition tells us that St. Dominic, a holy friar, played a role in the development of the Rosary. It's said that the Virgin Mary appeared to him and gave him the Rosary as a powerful tool to fight heresy and promote devotion to her and her Son, Jesus.

- **The Mysteries of the Rosary:**

The Rosary evolved to include the Mysteries we know today: the Joyful, Sorrowful, and Glorious Mysteries. These Mysteries focus on important moments in the lives of Jesus and Mary. They allow us to journey through their lives in prayer, deepening our connection with them.

- **Addition of the Luminous Mysteries:**

In 2002, Pope John Paul II added the Luminous Mysteries to the Rosary. These Mysteries, also called the "Mysteries of Light," help us meditate on events from Jesus' public life. They complete the story of His life and teachings.

The Mysteries of the Rosary are a treasured tradition within the Catholic faith. They are a way for us to connect with Jesus and Mary, to reflect on their love and sacrifice, and to draw nearer to God through prayer. These Mysteries are a source of comfort and strength for Catholics, guiding us on a spiritual journey of faith and love.

STEP BY STEP GUIDE FOR PRAYING THE ROSARY

20 minutes are required.

How to Pray the Rosary

1. Begin with the Cross Sign.

In the name of the Father, the Son, and the Holy Spirit. Amen

2. Pray the Apostles' Creed while holding the crucifix.

I believe in God, the Father almighty, the Creator of heaven and earth, and in Jesus Christ, His only Son, our Lord, who was conceived by the Holy Spirit, born of the Virgin Mary, suffered under Pontius Pilate, was crucified, died, and was buried; He descended into hell; He ascended into heaven, and is seated at the right hand of God the Father almighty; from there He will come to judge the living and the dead. I believe in the Holy Spirit, the Holy Catholic Church, the communion of saints, the forgiveness of sins, the bodily resurrection, and eternal life. Amen.

3. Pray an Our Father on the first bead.

Our Father who art in heaven; Hallowed be thy name, thy kingdom come; thy will be done on earth as it is in heaven. Give us our daily bread, and forgive us our transgressions as we forgive those who transgress against us; and lead us not into temptation, but rescue us from harm. Amen.

4. Pray a Hail Mary on each of the next three beads.

Hail Mary, full of grace; The Lord is with you, blessed are you among women, and blessed is the fruit of your womb, Jesus. Holy Mary, Mother of God, Pray for us sinners, now and at the hour of our death. Amen.

5. Pray a Glory Be on the next bead.

Glory be to the Father, the Son, and the Holy Spirit; as it was in the beginning, is now, and always will be. Amen.

6. Pray during the first decade.

Announce the secret on the huge bead, followed by an Our Father.

Say a Hail Mary on each of the ten little beads while continuing to contemplate the riddle.

Say the Glory Be at the end of the decade.

After that, say the **Fatima Prayer:**

Forgive us our sins, Jesus, and save us from the fires of hell; lead all souls to Heaven, especially those who are most in need of your kindness. Amen

7. Repeat this pattern over the next several decades.

10 Hail Marys -> Glory Be -> O my Jesus (Fatima Prayer)

8. Finish with the Hail Holy Queen after the 5 decades.

Hail, dear Queen, merciful mother of our life, sweetness, and hope. To you, poor expelled children of Eve, we wail; to you we sigh, mourning and weeping in this valley of tears.
Turn your mercy-filled eyes toward us, most gracious advocate, and after this, our exile, show us the blessed fruit of your womb, Jesus. O kind, loving, and sweet Virgin Mary.

O holy Mother of God, pray for us.
That we may be made worthy of Christ's promises.

9. Finish with the closing prayer.

Let us say a prayer:

O God, whose Only Begotten Son has purchased for us the rewards of eternal life through His Life, Death, and Resurrection, grant, we beseech thee, that while meditating on these mysteries of the most holy Rosary of the Blessed Virgin Mary, we may imitate what they contain and obtain what they promise, through the same Christ our Lord. Amen.

10. Finish with the Cross Sign.

In the name of the Father, the Son, and the Holy Spirit. Amen

PRAYERS SAID IN THE ROSARY

The Rosary devotion consists of various prayers, all of which are based on Scripture. You can learn about the traditional order of these prayers in the Rosary under "How to Pray: The Rosary" below.

The Apostles' Creed

"I believe in God, the Father almighty ..."

The Apostle's Creed is used to begin the Rosary. It is an appropriate way to begin this prayer, confirming our essential Catholic values. Each line is drawn from several books of the Bible, including the Gospels, 1 Peter, 1 Corinthians, Acts, and others.

Our Father

"Our Father in heaven, hallowed be your name …"

This prayer, often known as the Lord's Prayer, came directly from Jesus in Matthew 6, when he instructs his disciples how to pray.

All hail Mary!

"Hail Mary, full of grace …"

Although the repeated Hail Mary prayer is intended to Mary, the act of love is ultimately directed to Jesus, with her and through her.

The heart of the Rosary is the Hail Mary prayer. We pray ten Hail Marys in each of the five decades, for a total of 50 Hail Marys at the end of your devotion. This prayer, in which we request Mary's intercession, is also based on Scripture. The first two lines are from Luke's first chapter, when the Angel Gabriel announces Christ's arrival at the Annunciation and Mary's cousin, Elizabeth, greets Mary at the Visitation.

Glory Be

"Glory Be to the Father ..."

The Glory Be is also known as a doxology, which is a Greek word that means "an expression of praise or glory." This is a simple and popular prayer in which we ask that the Holy Trinity be exalted at all times.

The Fatima Prayer

"O my Jesus, forgive us our sins ..."

Mary herself delivered the Fatima Prayer to three shepherd children on July 13, 1917, during her apparition in Fatima, Portugal. We beseech Jesus for mercy on ourselves and all souls in this prayer, which is repeated at the conclusion of each decade.

Holy Queen, hail!

"Hail, Holy Queen, Mother of Mercy ..."

The Rosary concludes with this powerful prayer, which derives from the ancient practice of monks finishing community prayer with the Salve Regina (a Latin chant of the Hail, Holy Queen). We give gratitude to God for Mary's participation in all of the saving events of Jesus' life, death, and Resurrection, as we are reminded that Jesus is given to us through his Mother Mary.

THE MYSTERIES OF THE ROSARY

Each of the five decades of the Rosary focuses on a different aspect of the Paschal Mystery. Each of the four sets of mysteries — Joyful, Sorrowful, Luminous, and Glorious — incorporates five significant events from Jesus' life. We enter into one set of these mysteries at a time when saying the Rosary, pondering on them through the eyes of Mary, the disciple who was closest to Jesus and knew him best. On particular days of the week, the Church typically prays certain mysteries, as follows:

- Monday: Joyful Mystery
- Tuesday: Sorrowful Mystery
- Wednesday: Glorious Mystery
- Thursday: Luminous Mystery
- Friday: Sorrowful Mystery
- Saturday: Joyful Mystery
- Sunday: Glorious Mystery

Mysteries of Joy (Monday and Saturday)

The Joyful Mysteries inspire us to reflect on the Incarnation, and we are immersed in the awe of Jesus coming to earth as a baby. We see the incredible story unfold through Mary's eyes, from the appearance of the angel (The Annunciation) to the greeting of her cousin Elizabeth (The Visitation), the birth of her son (The Nativity), and the significant events that point to who this child is and what he will do (The Presentation and Finding in the Temple). We are encouraged to "reflect on them in [our] heart[s]" like Mary did (Luke 2:19).

Mysteries of Sorrow (Tuesday and Friday)

The Sorrowful Mysteries help us relieve Jesus' passion and death. We not only remember it, but we also enter it, keeping vigil with Jesus in his agony prior to his arrest (The Agony in the Garden). With The Scourging at the Pillar, The Crowning of Thorns, and The Carrying of the Cross... we enter into his agony, and then we stand at the foot of that cross alongside Mary as we witness his Crucifixion and Death. As we consider the cost of our salvation and redemption, we strive to comprehend the depths of God's love for us. We feel his sadness and regret even more intensely when we see it through his mother's eyes.

Luminous Mysteries (Thursday)

We reflect on the events of Jesus' public ministry through the Luminous Mysteries: his revelation as the Beloved Son of the Father at the Baptism in the Jordan, his first public miracle at the Wedding at Cana, his Proclamation of the Kingdom of God, Jesus' Transfiguration, and the Institution of the Eucharist at the Last Supper. "In the Luminous mysteries, apart from the miracle at Cana, the presence of Mary remains in the background," remarked Pope St. John Paul II. Nonetheless, the role she played at Cana follows Christ throughout his ministry. The revelation provided directly by the Father at the Jordan Baptism, echoed by John the Baptist, is placed on Mary's lips at Cana, and it becomes the great mother admonition that Mary gives to the Church of all ages: 'Do whatever he tells you.'"

Glorious Mysteries (Wednesday and Sunday)

In the Glorious Mysteries, we reflect on the amazing miracles that occur following Jesus' death. These events demonstrate that Jesus is who he claims to be: the Son of God. We feel the risen Christ's delight and see ourselves as Mary or the first disciples (The Resurrection). We see Jesus' ascension into heaven and the descent of the Holy Spirit at Pentecost while we pray. Though not expressly referenced in Scripture, the last two mysteries are built on hundreds of years of tradition based on passages from Revelation and Song of Songs. We commemorate the grace and role Jesus bestowed upon his mother (the Assumption and Coronation of Mary), and we hope that where Mary goes, we shall follow one day.

WHY DO WE RECITE THE ROSARY

Consider the Rosary to be like the ocean: There's something in it for everyone, whether you're an experienced mystic wishing to go deeper in prayer with our Lord, a novice attempting to understand how to pray, or someone asking the Lord's aid with something going on in your life right now. The deep-sea explorer and the youngster building sandcastles on the beach can both enjoy the same ocean at different levels. This is also true of the Rosary. The Rosary is a prayer for persons of all ages who are going through different life circumstances and may have varying levels of acquaintance with the devotion. The reason for the Rosary is straightforward: Mary was present during Christ's joyful, sorrowful, brilliant, and beautiful moments. So, with Mary's aid, we aim to grow closer to Christ by thinking on Jesus' life. We may choose to pray with Mary for a specific aim, or we may seek solace from the Blessed Mother and her Son. Any cause to pray the Rosary is a lovely one.

PRAYING THE ROSARY EVERY DAY

The Rosary can be prayed at any hour of day or night. While some choose to pray with beads, they are not required for our time with Jesus and Mary. Praying the whole Rosary takes between 15 - 25 minutes, but if you only have a few minutes, you can always do one decade (one Our Father, ten Hail Marys, and a Glory Be).

Consider the following prayer periods if you want to purposefully incorporate the Rosary into your daily prayer routine:

•If you go for daily walks, consider including the Rosary into your regimen.

•Pray the Rosary during your commute; listen and pray as you begin or end your workday.

•Pray while preparing dinner.

•Set aside some quiet time to pray as you prepare for the day or prepare to sleep.

Printed in Great Britain
by Amazon